The Late Poems
of Wang An-shih

OTHER BOOKS BY DAVID HINTON

Writing

Hunger Mountain (*essays*)
Fossil Sky (*poetry*)

Translation

I Ching: The Book of Change
The Four Chinese Classics
Classical Chinese Poetry: An Anthology
The Selected Poems of Wang Wei
The Mountain Poems of Meng Hao-jan
Mountain Home: The Wilderness Poetry of Ancient China
The Mountain Poems of Hsieh Ling-yün
Tao Te Ching
The Selected Poems of Po Chü-i
The Analects
Mencius
Chuang Tzu: The Inner Chapters
The Late Poems of Meng Chiao
The Selected Poems of Li Po
The Selected Poems of T'ao Ch'ien
The Selected Poems of Tu Fu

The Late Poems
of Wang An-shih

Translated from the Chinese by David Hinton

A NEW DIRECTIONS BOOK

Manufactured in the United States of America
New Directions Books are printed on acid-free paper
First published as a New Directions Paperbook (NDP1302) in 2015

Library of Congress Cataloging-in-Publication Data
Wang, Anshi, 1021–1086.
[Poems. Selections. English]
The late poems of Wang An-shih / translated by David Hinton.
pages cm
Includes bibliographical references.
ISBN 978-0-8112-2263-1 (alk. paper)
I. Hinton, David, 1954– translator. II. Title.
PL2686.A2 2015
895.11'4—dc23   2014032863

10 9 8 7 6 5 4 3 2 1

New Directions Books are published for James Laughlin
by New Directions Publishing Corporation
80 Eighth Avenue, New York 10011
ndbooks.com

Acknowledgments

Translation of this book was made possible by the generous
financial support of the following institutions:

THE CULLMAN CENTER FOR SCHOLARS AND WRITERS

THE NATIONAL ENDOWMENT FOR THE ARTS

Contents

Introduction   xiii

Middle years   3

Sent to a Monk   3

Written on a Wall at the Monastery Where I've Stayed . . .   4

Sitting Still on a Spring Day   4

Visiting River-Serene   5

Written on a Wall at Samadhi-Forest Monastery   5

Steady-Shield Monastery   6

Thinking of a Dream   7

Wandering Bell Mountain   7

Written on a Window at Samadhi-Forest Monastery   8

I rollick   8

Here, Now   9

Autumn Night   10

Who's infusing   11

Here at Bell Mountain   11

Accord All-Gather Comes Through Snow to Visit   12

Following thoughts   12

Here at River-Serene   13

East Ridge   13

Wandering Out with a Full Moon to Eightfold-Integrity River   14

In My Words-Bright Library at Samadhi-Forest Monastery   15

East River   15

Self-Portrait   16

Self-Portrait   16

Death of My Horse   17

In bamboo forest   17

A Lone Kindred-Tree   18

Sent to Candor-Sky   19

At Manifest-Tao Spring   19

Across a thousand   20

Flourish Time-worn and I Wander Beguiled and Never Meet   20

Dream   21

Inviting Integrity-Met to Visit   21

Returning Home from Bell Mountain at Dusk, Sent to a Monk   22

Talking with Manifest Sky-Ascent   23

Early Autumn   23

At the Shrine-Tower of Ch'an Master Lumen-Serene   24

Pondering My Host at Orchid-Gift Creek   24

Following the Rhymes of Pattern-Unraveled's Poem . . .   25

Golden-Tomb City   26

Song for Grain   26

At the Palace Gardens in River-Serene, Sent to Origin-Across   27

In Jest on Bell Mountain, Given to Adept Gather-Grain   28

River   28

Five willows   29

Sent to Jewel-Awake   29

Sent to Assistant Magistrate Guide-Bell   30

Sent to Abbot Whole-Quiet   30

Thinking of Golden-Tomb City Long Ago   31

Parting in River-Serene   33

On a Farewell Journey to Send off Mend-Source . . .   33

Climbing Up to Treasure-Master's Grave-Shrine   34

Drifting South Creek   35

Again at South-Creek Tower, Written on a Wall   35

On a moonlit island bridge   36

Written on Master Lake-Shadow's Wall   36

Napping at noon   37

Written on a Wall at Balance-Peace Post-Station   37

Spring Rain   38

Looking at a Painting of Lumen Island   38

Above the Yangtze   39

Leaving the City   39

After *Clouds Limitless* by a Monk at Nirvana-Radiant . . .   40

There's a Huge Pine Beside the Road, and People Think . . .   41

Sun west and low   41

Off-Hand Poem   42

Spirit creatures   42

Radiance-Hut   43

Life at Samadhi-Forest Monastery   44

Written on Eightfold-Integrity River   44

Farewell to Gaze-Arrive   45

With my goosefoot staff   45

Suddenly   46

Above the Yangtze   46

Wandering at Delight-Mind Pavilion . . .   47

Anchored on Abandon River   48

A Spring Day   48

Just to Say   49

After Elder-Ease's Poem *Buddha-Wind Ch'in*   49

Listening to Floodwater Past Midnight   50

On Tower Heights   50

Following Apricot-Blossom Rhymes   51

Spring Skies Clear   51

Sent to Abbot Whole-Repose   52

A Country Walk   53

Pure-Apparent Monastery   53

Cricket Weaving-Song   54

On this side, flood-strewn   54

Ninth Month, Yi Year of the Snake, On Climbing . . .   55

River Rain   56

Written on a Wall at Source-Aware Monastery's . . .   56

At Broken-Tomb Shores   57

Farewell to Candor-Achieve   58

Winter-Solstice Sacrifice   58

The Ancient Pine   59

Late Spring   60

In Jest, Sent to Abbot Empty-White   60

At Dragon-Spring Monastery's Stone Well   61

At the Shrine-Hut on Eightfold-Integrity River   62

Wandering Bell Mountain   62

Autumn Wind   63

Farewell at the River Tower   64

Bell Mountain   64

Meeting an Old Friend a Splendor-Hoard Monastery   65

A Moonlit Night in Mid-Autumn, Sent to Broad-Origin . . .   66

South of Town, Leaving   66

This Spirit-Vulture Mountain   67

Farewell to a Monk Leaving for Heaven-Terrace Mountain   67

Parting in River-Serene   68

Following Prosper Bright-Gather's Rhymes   68

Following the Rhymes of Abbot Elder-Guide's Poem . . .   69

Thoughts on Bell Mountain   70

Plum Blossoms Along the Canal   70

Skies Clearing   71

Hair white   71

Thoughts Sent on My Way Home from River-Serene . . .   72

Following the Rhymes of a Poem Sent by Encompass-Anew   73

A Friend in Mourning Visits River-Serene   73

Recognizing Myself   74

The Ancient Monastery   75

Sent to the Painter, Sage-Cloud, in River-Serene   75

Summer Night on a Boat, Chill in the Air   76

On mountain slopes   77

At the Mouth of Lumen River   77

Drifting Grain-Thresh River   78

Old now, tangled   78

Written on a Wall at Half-Mountain Monastery   79

Poking Fun at My White Hair   80

White Hair's Answer   80

Above the River   81

On the Terrace, for Mind-Source   83

Gazing North   83

I can't see anything of this autumn day   84

Reading History   85

Chants   86

Thoughts as I Lie Alone   87

Cut Flowers   88

Notes   89
Finding List   98
Sources   105

Introduction

Wang An-shih (王安石: 1021–1086 C.E.) was an eccentric figure of magisterial proportions. He devoted himself to government service until the age of fifty-five, becoming one of the most powerful and controversial statesman in Chinese history. But even as he rose to become Prime Minister, he remained frugal almost to a fault and completely immune, even hostile, to the grandeur of high office and political power. He worked tirelessly to improve the lives of commoners, and was so preoccupied with this work that he sometimes forgot to bathe or eat. His unkempt hair and clothes appalled many colleagues, and his behavior often offended them, for he had little patience with the decorum of social niceties, avoided the obligatory parties and banquets, and didn't hesitate to criticize his superiors. Still, he was a daunting intellectual force who elicited deep respect, even among those who objected to his unconventional ways.

Eventually Wang retired to the life of a recluse poet and spent his last decade wandering among the mountains and Ch'an (Zen) Buddhist monasteries of southeast China, writing the poetry that made him one of the greatest poets in a great poetic age: the Sung Dynasty. His eccentricity continued. Completely absorbed in his literary pursuits and Ch'an practice, Wang remained unconcerned with his appearance. Indeed, he was easily mistaken for a local peasant, and became famous for riding disheveled and aimless across the countryside on his donkey (rather than the elegant horse expected for a man of his stature).

This strange figure, part peasant and part Prime Minister, wrote a particularly distilled and philosophical poetry. Although full of everyday things, these poems inhabit consciousness and landscape at the deepest cosmological levels. "Vast and silent, / western mountains hover between Presence and Absence," reports one poem. And another:

> Through a thousand, ten thousand peaks,
> this road between Presence and Absence
>
> wanders. Bees sampling open blossoms,
> gibbons climbing trees to dine on fruit . . .

Absence and Presence are the two fundamental elements in the cosmology of Lao Tzu's *Tao Te Ching* (ca. 6th century B.C.E.), the seminal Taoist text that first articulated the philosophical framework shared by the artist-intellectuals who created classical Chinese culture. Presence is simply the empirical universe, which the ancients described as the ten thousand living and nonliving things in constant transformation, and Absence the generative emptiness from which this ever-changing realm of Presence perpetually emerges. Lao Tzu called this cosmological process Tao (道), or Way, and he described it as female in nature, for his was a primal cosmology oriented around earth's mysterious generative force.

Wang An-shih famously reinterpreted a key passage in the *Tao Te Ching* to emphasize these deep cosmological dimensions. For fifteen hundred years, the passage had been read:

> Free of perennial desire, you see mystery,
> and full of perennial desire, you see appearance.

As there is no punctuation in classical Chinese texts, readers must decide where to place pauses (not unlike our commas and periods) as they read. Differences in placement could create dramatically different readings. Wang read these lines with the caesura in a different place, creating a new reading that became standard throughout the centuries that followed:

> In perennial Absence, you see mystery,
> and in perennial Presence, you see appearance.

This couplet appears in the *Tao Te Ching*'s first chapter, which is a concise outline of Lao Tzu's cosmology, and reads like this with Wang's new reading of that crucial couplet:

> A Tao called Tao isn't the perennial Tao.
> A name that names isn't the perennial name:
>
> the named is mother to the ten thousand things,
> but the unnamed is origin to all heaven and earth.

In perennial Absence, you see mystery,
and in perennial Presence, you see appearance.

Though the two are one and the same,
once they arise, they differ in name.

One and the same they're called *dark-enigma,*
dark-enigma deep within dark-enigma,

gateway of all mystery.

Absence is often referred to as "emptiness" (空 or 虛), and it is described as the generative void from which the ten thousand things (Presence) are born and to which they return. Our language and intellectual assumptions have trained us to interpret such terms—Absence, emptiness, void—as a kind of non-material metaphysical realm in contrast to the material realm of Presence. We instinctively want to interpret Absence and Presence as a dualistic pair, in which Presence is the physical universe and Absence is a kind of metaphysical womb from which the physical emerges. But this kind of dualism was foreign to ancient China's artist-intellectuals, who followed after Lao Tzu's seminal poem above, where he says of Absence and Presence that "the two are one and the same." They were thoroughgoing empiricists. Absence is emptiness only in the sense that it is empty of particular forms. It is reality seen as one undifferentiated tissue, while Presence is reality seen in its differentiated forms, the ten thousand things. From this it follows that Absence and Presence are not two separate realms, but are instead a single tissue.

For the ancient Chinese, the most majestic and complete manifestation of this cosmology was the realm of rivers and mountains. It is there in countless paintings from the landscape tradition: the pregnant emptiness in the form of vacant rivers and lakes, mist and sky; and the mountain landscape as it emerges from that emptiness and hovers, peopled sparsely, seemingly on the verge of vanishing back into the emptiness. The Tao of a Chinese sage was to dwell as an organic part of this cosmological process, and Wang was a consummate master of this dwelling in his later years: his life as a recluse among those rivers and mountains, his cultivation of Taoist and Ch'an Buddhist insight, his poetic practice.

As is clear from his many poems about monasteries and Ch'an Buddhist life, Wang An-shih was a devoted practitioner of Ch'an. But rather than exploring doctrinal Buddhist poetry, his work uses the Ch'an context as a way of giving immediate experience surprising philosophical depths. Ch'an's evolution in China began around 400 C.E. as an amalgam of Taoist and Buddhist thought. Ch'an clarified anew the spiritual ecology of early Taoist thought, focusing within that philosophical framework on meditation, Ch'an's central way of fathoming reality at a level that lies beyond words. By Wang's time six hundred years later, Taoist/Ch'an thought defined the mental framework of virtually all artist-intellectuals. Ch'an meditation allows one to watch as Presence emerges from Absence in the form of thought burgeoning forth from emptiness and then disappearing back into it, thereby revealing that the subjective and objective realms are part of the same tissue. Delving deeper into meditative practice, once the restless train of thought falls silent, one simply dwells in that undifferentiated emptiness, that generative realm of Absence.

Once the self and its constructions of the world dissolve into the emptiness of Absence, what remains is empty consciousness itself, known in Ch'an terminology as "empty mind" or "no-mind"—a concept that recurs in Wang An-shih's poetry. As Absence, empty mind attends to the ten thousand things with mirror-like clarity, and so the act of perception becomes a spiritual act: empty mind mirroring the world, leaving its ten thousand things utterly simple, utterly themselves, and utterly sufficient. Hence, the ten thousand things replace thought and even identity itself. This weave of consciousness and world is the heart of sage-dwelling as part of the Taoist/Ch'an cosmology. Few Chinese poets explore this dwelling with as much philosophical intensity and directness as Wang. In his poems, Wang describes mind-depths that are empty, or quiet as a mountain peak; wind rinses his ten-thousand-mile long river-and-lake mind away; he looks out and feels mountains and valleys enter his eyes; the moon is his friend for wandering one day, and on another it lights up his thoughts.

But it goes even deeper than this, weaving consciousness and landscape together at the most fundamental levels, and those depths depend on the remarkable resources of the Chinese poetic language: its texture of imagistic clarity, pictographic script, and grammatical emptiness. As illustration, one might choose from Wang An-shih's poems almost at random:

A Spring Day

I gaze into moss at my brushwood gate, rainwater radiant,
then wander through spring, blossoms crowding branches

everywhere. People travel distant roads and never arrive,
but all day here, birds in song leave and come back again.

Those depths appear first in the pictographic nature of the language: thought made of things themselves. Although these pictographic images are stylized and simplified and combined with phonetic elements, the erudite intellectuals of ancient China were very aware of them as the basic texture of the language. In the poem's first line, for example, we find poetic thinking constructed from a whole world of pictographic imagery, of things in and of themselves:

柴	門	照	水	見	青	苔
brushwood	gate	shine	water	see/appear	green	moss

Beneath highly stylized images of a foot and a person at the top, 柴 contains the picture of a tree at the bottom, deriving from the early form 木, showing a tree's trunk, with roots below and branches above. 門 portrays a traditional courtyard gate with a pair of doors mounted on pivots, seen more clearly in oracle-bone forms such as: 門. 照 contains most crucially the images for sun (日, which appears in oracle-bones as ☉) and fire (灬, abbreviated form of 火, which is a simplified version of earlier fire images such as this oracle-bone rendering: 火). The graph also includes, in the upper right, pictures of a knife blade and a mouth. The early version of 水 was 水, which depicts the rippling water of a river or stream. 見 is the picture of an eye (目, derived from the oracle-bone 目) atop a profile view of a person walking (人). The top half of 青 portrays a sprout, deriving from early images such as 生, and the bottom image apparently began as the earth or field from which the sprout grows: 青. 苔 begins at the top with the grass radical, an image of grass shoots, rendered in early script as: 艸. And the bottom half depicts a mouth with breath coming out, which is more clearly visible in this early version of the graph: 台.

Perhaps even more profound is how the minimal and wide-open grammar allows a number of simultaneous readings, all of which weave identity into natural process. The most straightforward reading of this line in terms of pure grammar is something like: "At the brushwood gate, lit water sees green moss." This is a plausible interpretation because pooled water has a mirrored surface that could be described as "seeing" green moss; and there are philosophical reasons for such a statement (see below). A second reading is suggested by two facts about the Chinese poetic language: seven-word lines like this always have a grammatical pause after the fourth word, and first-person subjects are very often absent. In this reading, an "I" is added after the fourth word: "At the brushwood gate, beside lit water, [I] see green moss." But in English, the most profound dimension of this reading is lost. Adding the subject pronoun that English grammar requires injects a Western spirit-center into the poem, a problem that cannot be resolved without resort to a strange experimental English inappropriate to these poems, and so inevitably recurs throughout these translations. But in the Chinese, identity remains an absent presence because the "I" is not actually there in the line. This weaves identity into the empirical world around it; and at the same time, it reveals the actual experience of perception, as revealed through meditation, where one can see that mirror-deep perception is without self-identity.

Still water is a common metaphor in ancient China for an enlightened mind because, like still water, a profound and empty mind possesses shadowy depths, mirrored clarity, and the absence of thought and self-identity. This suggests another reading of the line: "A lit pool of water at the brushwood gate, [I] see green moss." And finally, the vanishing of self-identity that weaves consciousness and empirical world together in these simultaneous readings is deepened further by the fact that 見 means not only "to see," but also "to appear." Interpreting 見 this way, one finds identity erased and the line becomes: "At the brushwood gate, in lit water, green moss appears," which in terms of empty mind is hardly different from: "At the brushwood gate, in my mind, green moss appears."

Wang's second line also erases the separation of self and landscape:

春	遠	花	枝	漫	漫	開
spring	wander	blossoms	branches	brimming/ spreading	brimming/ spreading	open

Here, the grammar offers several simultaneous possibilities: "Spring wanders branch-blossoms open everywhere far and wide," "Branch-blossoms wander spring, open everywhere far and wide," and "I wander spring where branch-blossoms open everywhere far and wide." These readings come together in empty mind, where spring and its blossoms are mirrored deeply, becoming the content of consciousness wholly, so when "I" wander they too wander. And finally, 開 at the end of the line describes both blossoms opening and consciousness opening.

As the poem continues, it raises the question of arrival: "People travel distant roads and never arrive." Wang goes on to suggest that he has already arrived, which is exactly what the first couplet in all its complexity describes: dwelling as an ongoing and profound arrival without the need of going anywhere, dwelling as part of Tao. The final line states this with what seems like a metaphor: "All day here, birds in song leave and come back again." But the empty mind suffusing the poem makes it much more than a metaphor, because that mirror-deep empty mind erases any distinction between subjective and objective realms. As with the lit pool in line one and the blossoms in line two, the birds are the very content of the poet's consciousness, and so their arrival is no different from his arrival, his dwelling at such depths there in his courtyard on an ordinary spring day late in life.

This cultivation of Taoist/Ch'an spiritual depth represents one side of the ancient Chinese artist-intellectual. The other side is a Confucian responsibility to help the emperor care for his people by working in government. Given his accomplishment as a poet, it is surprising that Wang spent most of his life fulfilling this Confucian responsibility. Though he earned a national reputation for his scholarship and administrative abilities during his younger years in government service, Wang was never anxious to be involved in the pomp and circumstance of life in the central government at the capital. Instead, he held a number of regional positions near River-Serene (Chiang-ning: present day Nanjing), one of southeast China's major cities. Wang's father was an official posted in River-Serene at the time of his death, when Wang was eighteen, and afterward the family adopted River-Serene as their home. Wang's positions there kept him close not only to his hometown but also to mountain landscapes and Ch'an monasteries, where he often associated with monks.

At the age of thirty-three, Wang finally took a position in the capital, where he slowly rose through increasingly important positions. He wrote some poetry in those years, mostly rather mediocre poems of political and social commentary, a reflection of his passionate preoccupation with government work, though he occasionally wrote poems exploring his Taoist/Ch'an interests. China was enjoying a long period of relative peace and prosperity, but there were unresolved issues that increasingly threatened society: constant struggles with "barbarian" invasions, together with unsustainable military expenditures; growing impoverishment of farmers and small merchants; inadequate tax structure, and so on. Serious reforms were widely considered necessary if the government was to sustain its accomplishments. Wang sent a petition to the emperor, his famous "Ten-Thousand-Word Petition," which outlined his political theory and a wholesale restructuring of government and society. It made him an instant celebrity among advocates of reform, but the emperor didn't act on his recommendations.

Wang's mother died when he was forty-two, and he returned to River-Serene for the traditional three-year mourning period. Toward the end of that time, a reform-minded emperor came to power, and he appointed Wang provincial-governor in River-Serene. Knowing Wang's reputation, this Emperor Shen-tsung summoned him to the capital, appointing him an imperial scholar and advisor. Wang soon became the emperor's most trusted advisor, serving first as Grand Councilor, one of three ruling ministers, then as Prime Minister, the most powerful person in China other than the emperor. In fact, Shen-tsung was only twenty-one, and he generally allowed Wang to guide him in developing policy. Wang threw himself into his work with great intensity. Indeed, he instituted a wholesale reform of society during those years, the most radical restructuring in pre-modern history, hoping to resolve the nation's structural problems and improve the lives of common people.

Wang's reforms were guided by strict pragmatism and a belief that if the common people are prosperous and happy the country as a whole will flourish. The reforms were exhaustive and complex, involving every aspect of society—economy, agriculture, military, education, taxation, law, trade—and they were fiercely opposed by many in the government who were committed to the status quo and the interests of a wealthy and powerful aristocracy. Indeed, it seems that where the reforms stumbled, it was usually due to obstruction from these opponents. It is a testament to Wang's self-assurance and independence of mind that although he faced withering criticism from colleagues on a daily basis, he continued to move his reforms forward. Nevertheless, the strain of work and relentless criticism did wear him down, causing him to retire once for much of a year, during which he returned to serve as provincial-governor at River-Serene.

At the age of fifty-five, after eight years as the emperor's chief advisor and policy-maker, Wang had his reforms securely in place. He felt he had fulfilled his Confucian responsibility with great success and was therefore free to pursue his deepest passion: a Taoist/Ch'an self-cultivation centered on poetic practice. So he left the government in the hands of trusted compatriots and retired to a reclusive life in the countryside near River-Serene. He was initially appointed provincial-governor in River-Serene again, but his true desire is revealed by the fact that he chose to live at Samadhi-Forest, a Ch'an monastery on his beloved Bell Mountain. He soon resigned the governorship and began his years as a recluse, moving to a simple house he called "Half-Mountain" because it was halfway between the city and Bell Mountain, meaning it was about an hour's walk to either destination.

In addition to his poetic practice, Wang spent those later years engaged in intensive scholarly work, producing many volumes of commentaries on traditional classics and Buddhist sutras, as well as a grand etymological dictionary that probed the philosophical dimensions revealed by the pictographic histories of ideograms. At the same time, he was practicing Ch'an Buddhism and wandering the mountains around his home, a Taoist/Ch'an cultivation of the rivers-and-mountains realm that shapes his poems. Sometimes he would go to the mountains, stay in Ch'an monasteries and wander the landscape; other times he would leave his house riding a donkey with a bag of books and flatbread, and wander with no destination or purpose in mind.

Wang's reforms remained in place during his years of retirement. But however satisfying that must have been, he was haunted by wide-spread opposition to those reforms, opposition that steadily undermined their effectiveness. Wang suffered from a string of health problems during these years, including a major stroke at the age of sixty-three. Soon thereafter he gave his Half-Mountain house to the Ch'an community for use as a monastery and moved into the city. The following year, nine years after Wang's retirement from politics, Emperor Shen-tsung died, and Wang had to watch helplessly as conservative elements dismantled his reforms.

Over the centuries since his death, literary history has recognized Wang An-shih as one of China's greatest poets. But political history was not so kind. Political history is written by the rich and powerful, exactly those people whom Wang's reforms offended. Forty years after Wang's death, northern China was lost to "barbarian" invaders, and for centuries Wang and his radical ideas were blamed for the catastrophe. Only recently have historians and political thinkers begun to see Wang as a courageous and pragmatic reformer whose policies had the potential to make society work for the common people rather than just the privileged few. At the end of his life, Wang was already seeing himself demonized by history-makers (see "Reading History" on p. 85). Heartsick and struggling with illness, Wang endured the death of his wife and then, at the age of sixty-five, he passed away.

In dramatic contrast to his stature as the most powerful statesman in China, Wang's reputation as a poet is based on the short landscape poems he wrote during his last ten years. The larger the poem, the larger the interpretive structure it imposes on the landscape of reality. Such is the case in the West, where a human-centered worldview has meant that great poems traditionally tended to be large, often epic in their proportions, subsuming the ten thousand things within their human concerns. Quite the opposite, China's great poetry tends to be short, typically eight or four lines, and Wang specialized in the latter: the Ch'an-inspired quatrain, which is the most concise of China's poetic forms. As a statesman, Wang worked hard to impose order on a recalcitrant political system, but the brief poems Wang wrote late in life dwell in a place of mystery and insight. Rather than subsuming the world within human preoccupations or imposing a human order on the world, his late poems open an emptiness where consciousness is woven into landscape and its ten thousand things. And the fact that a man of such majestic public stature would focus on such poems is an indication of the grandeur inherent in that humble gesture.

The Late Poems
of Wang An-shih

Middle years

Middle years devoted to the nation, I lived a fleeting dream.
Home again now in old age, I wander borderland wilderness:

five lakes, spring grasses. Gazing into far mountains, it's clear
I'm not alone. Those peaks crowd my little-boat life cast adrift.

Sent to a Monk

Through ten scattered years all confusion tangled among
affairs of the world, I masked my haggard look in smiles.

If you want a mind peaceful as autumn waters, you live
your life idle as cloud drifting ranges of mountain peaks.

Written on a Wall at the Monastery Where I've Stayed Since Quitting My Illustrious Job

An old adept living among mountain forests, I sit *ch'an*
stillness. My mind's rinsed suddenly clear now, leaving

that self I am out along dream's frontier, where it stays.
Maybe next spring, at festival time, I'll go looking for it.

Sitting Still on a Spring Day

Ten years cascaded away before I left for home, then every
river seen and mountain climbed was a new way of thinking.

Here facing wine, these hundred thousand depths of longing,
I can't bear stricken cries of mountain partridge setting out.

Visiting River-Serene

I've traveled this land five times in seven years, and at last
laugh in wonder. It's such majesty to be alive in this world,

to become another bundle of dry grain stored up, a lone old
man somehow sharing the idleness of generations to come.

Written on a Wall at
Samadhi-Forest Monastery

Samadhi-Forest has a host, the abbot,
and I'm the guest. Host and guest, we

each have our own mind, but they're
both quiet as the same mountain peak.

Steady-Shield Monastery

The Buddha hall's gold streamers trail off into clarities of idleness.
Wandering the pool, kingfisher-green ripples are written at depths.

Silk floss floats in thousands among motionless willow branches,
lotus leaves leaning into each other, hiding ten thousand shadows.

In vast mountain silences, summit clouds tumble over one another,
and on the river, fluttering sand-ducks drift and dive as they like.

Delighting in this, all thought of return forgotten, I grow patient,
a guest facing west wind to study the distances of its chant beyond.

Thinking of a Dream

The moon in a thousand rivers remains always a single moon,
but a master of Tao never scatters among the crowd of people.

Bell Mountain north and south: what makes this *ch'an* country?
Incense alight now and some distant time shares the same flame.

Wandering Bell Mountain

Gazing all day into mountains, I can't get enough of mountains.
Retire into mountains, and old age takes the form of mountains:

when mountain blossoms scatter away, mountains always remain,
and in empty mountain streamwater, mountains deepen idleness.

Written on a Window at Samadhi-Forest Monastery

Bamboo-partridge cry out, waking me from ancient Bright-
Distance dreamland. I rise, snuff out heat-stove and lamp.

When I ask the master what he dreamed last night, he says
simply: *It's all lost and forgotten, and who can speak of Absence?*

I rollick

I rollick through wildflower grasses,
sit alone on reed-crush cushions all

thatch-hut quiet. Old sun, treasured
guest, is it this good where you live?

Here, Now

1

Clouds rise out of Bell Mountain,
then vanish into Bell Mountain

peaks. Just ask mountain monks
about the place clouds are now.

2

Clouds appear out of no-mind,
then vanish back into no-mind

depths, no-mind no place to seek.
Not seeking is no-mind's place.

Autumn Night

I doze, a guest among topsy-turvy books,
then sit amid insect song. Isolate silence,

remnant lamp casting halos of darkness,
heavy dew settling across cold branches:

it's joy absolute to gaze out all idleness,
or even more, to sit deep *ch'an* stillness,

and it's beyond insight. I clamp my nose,
and chant in a long-ago sage's lost voice.

Who's infusing

Who's infusing spring tides with black-rock eye-liner,
teasing out gold, braiding it through willow branches?

From here to sunset peaks and sunrise seas, it's perfect
everywhere. However far I go, I never leave distances.

Here at Bell Mountain

Water soundless, a wandering stream skirts bamboo forest.
West of bamboo, wildflowers trace spring's tender assent.

Facing all this beneath thatch eaves, I sit through the day:
Not a single bird. No song. Mountain quiet goes deeper still.

Accord All-Gather Comes Through Snow to Visit

Abandoning books, I left for a life among ancient mountain forests,
no more searching for reasons, mind far from the world's dramas.

Suddenly, an old friend out for the snow arrives in my jade-white
courtyard. We talk and talk, answering his deepest search and mine.

Following thoughts

Following thoughts all brush-bramble my hands open through,
I trace ridgelines, cross creeks, climb out onto terraces beyond:

the simplest wind-and-dew bridge, a little-boat moon cast adrift,
and birds widowed or lost, their comings and goings at an end.

Here at River-Serene

Each time forests are lost to night, dawn's more startling still.
People somewhere call back and forth, a hundred kinds of noise

on spring wind. I leave my brushwood gate closed. That busy
world far away here, it's easy: birds seen become thoughts felt.

East Ridge

Together we climb this East Ridge lookout on New Year's Eve
and gaze at the Star River, its length lighting distant forests.

Earth's ten thousand holes cry and moan. That wind's our ruin,
and in a thousand seething waves, there's no trace of a heart.

Wandering Out with a Full Moon to Eightfold-Integrity River

Thoughts turned far away from you,
confusion rife, I can't sleep. Finally

I rise, gaze up into bright stars, then
saddle a horse and wander the road

east, thinking rivers and mountains
might ease my worries. I know you

ate no dinner. Come: we'll ladle out
clouds together here at their source.

In My Words-Bright Library
at Samadhi-Forest Monastery

I'm a traveler from such mountain
depths. How is it I have this name?

Leave a *ch'in* unplayed, and no one
fathoms how it's flawed or flawless.

East River

East River's swollen current surges around fallen trees.
Yellow reeds all cut, island shallows open away, empty.

In late light at South Creek, smoke rises. Vast and silent,
western mountains hover between Presence and Absence.

Self-Portrait

It's all mirage illusion, like cinnabar-and-azure paintings, this
human world. We wander here for a time, then vanish into dust.

Things aren't other than they are. That's all anyone can know.
Don't ask if this thing I am today is the thing I was long ago.

Self-Portrait

Things aren't other than they are.
I am today whoever I was long ago,

and if I can be described, it's as this
pure likeness of things themselves.

Death of My Horse

In loving devotion to this old guest among pine and bamboo, it
slept nights beneath my east window how many years? A colt

come from heaven's stable, it's turned dragon now and set out,
leaving only a lame little donkey for my wanderings in idleness.

In bamboo forest

In bamboo forest, my thatch hut's among stone cliff-roots.
Out front, through thin bamboo, you can see a village, but

I doze all day, all idleness, and no one stops by for a visit:
just this spring wind come sweeping my gate-path clean.

A Lone Kindred-Tree

Infused with elemental heaven's flourishing,
isolate and towering thousands of feet high

through mist, it never bows to circumstance.
Earthbound, its origins in empty mind abide

where ancient roots still grow full and strong,
leaves ablaze with *yang* and full of *yin*-dark.

In lit moments of clarity, thought impossible
to explain, I imagine carving a 5-string *ch'in*.

Sent to Candor-Sky

I follow a creek, goosefoot walking-stick in hand, then set out
across bridges. Can anyone share autumn's depths of crystalline

quiet? I linger on East Ridge and wonder, wonder. Here, it's all
ravaged grasses, clouds gone cold, evening distances, distances.

At Manifest-Tao Spring

It's been ages since I visited city markets,
and I'm past worry over disappointments.

It's quiet. I gather blossoms, and awaiting
sage-masters, drink clouds at their source.

Across a thousand

Across a thousand hundred-twist trails through forest hills,
a painting's wind-mist silvers autumn into a single color,

nothing left but the beauty of wandering out impulse here.
Red poplar-tears: what grief scatters them across streams?

Flourish Time-worn and I Wander
Beguiled and Never Meet

We set out, drift and wander wherever our beguiled whims take us,
no need to pretend our walking-sticks might meet at some bridge.

When *ch'an* mind opens, you can't ignore all this quiet emptiness.
And even old, with our crystalline bones of Tao, why fear the cold?

Dream

Knowing lifetimes are like dream, I search for nothing now.
Searching for nothing, a mind is perfectly empty, perfectly

quiet, and so deep in dream it traces borderlands of dream
clear through river and shoreline sands to the end of dream.

Inviting Integrity-Met to Visit

Grown old in mountain forests, tired of all our scattered
confusion, I lie around gazing at clouds, thinking of you.

They're perfect masters of no-mind, and still leave peaks
easily. Don't try to say you're more idle even than clouds.

Returning Home from Bell Mountain
at Dusk, Sent to a Monk

Through a thousand, ten thousand peaks,
this road between Presence and Absence

wanders. Bees sampling open blossoms,
gibbons climbing trees to dine on fruit,

I search for the way across a cold creek,
hoping dusk will light the journey home.

But the sky's soon dark, moonless, and
my houseboy's long since closed the gate.

Talking with Manifest Sky-Ascent

A pauper married a ravishing woman and lived out a life of
wealth and renown, all in a dream while the millet cooked.

Life's ten thousand events vanish like bird-flight empty in sky.
Why insist on clinging to what little you can still remember?

Early Autumn

Overnight rain purifies royal parkland.
Morning sun exalts the imperial city.

In good years, all harvest joy, people
dance on gravemounds, music pulsing.

At the Shrine-Tower of Ch'an Master Lumen-Serene

To clarify old age, he returned to these yellow-clay paths,
and now he's a dark-abyss master grown old, hair white.

Of thirty years and more, life's hundred worries, all that
remains are mountain-forest and wildflower-grass traces.

Pondering My Host at Orchid-Gift Creek

How many pines tower above Orchid-Gift Creek? How
many peaks rise north and south, east and west? I came

here days ago, but I'm still looking for this person sitting
ch'an stillness beside me, settled deep in his own nature.

Following the Rhymes of Pattern-Unraveled's Poem *Here in the Small Garden*

Birds no longer sing among courtyard walls and open rooms,
so much beauty, and frogs no longer call in garden pools. Now

trees cling to overnight rain, stained with autumn's first reds,
and wildflower grasses, green as ever, flare in morning sun.

The ten thousand things, heaven's loom of origins: there's no
loss or gain, it's true, but who welcomes the worry of this life?

Let's go out, walking-sticks in hand, and gaze into all change
itself—wondering, wondering, eyes become offerings of light.

Golden-Tomb City

Old lichen and moss: what more remains of Golden-Tomb,
where people came and went, wandering north and south?

Spring wind past stone walls remembers best: home after
home, apricot and peach in broken courtyards blossoming.

Song for Grain

Grain above the terrace: it's exquisite.
I gaze, and it darkens confusion away.

I must know a poet's *ch'i*-mind. How
else could I share this joy of the field?

At the Palace Gardens in River-Serene, Sent to Origin-Across

Painted boats sail through river distances north and south.
Night falls. I stroll bamboo thickets in my simple headcloth,

wander the Moon Terrace's kingfisher-and-emerald beauty.
Meanwhile, someone sneaks down side-streets heading east.

In Jest on Bell Mountain, Given to Adept Gather-Grain

Nursing ruins of age on southern paths, I gaze into old catalpas.
There are lanterns pouring everywhere like stars across earth,

but it's the sacred chants that are strange, tearing at wind-rinsed
land. Who understands *ch'an* adepts gone this deep into night?

River

When a spirit-spring broke open, it began
swelling and coiling on ahead and through

mountains crowded up, blocking the way.
It keeps flowing right on time to the sea,

harboring bright pearls in mud and sand,
frolicking dragons in cloud-and-rain dark.

Why ask where all its depths came from?
River gods see no further than themselves.

Five willows

Five willows and a mulberry-brush house,
thatch refuge beneath three-aspen whites:

wandering between them, pure boredom,
I suddenly see green-azure in green-azure!

Sent to Jewel-Awake

Morning fire, sunlit window, a bowl of rice gruel: mirror
quiet of a pond no fish troubles, we face each other, then

leave sage temples and mountain forests far behind, our
farewell a *ch'an* sky, its clarity a place we dwell together.

Sent to Assistant Magistrate Guide-Bell

You hurry around your life, and I just idle through mine,
so how could we ever wander up Bell Mountain together?

Outside city gates, I keep a child's routine. But turning to
look back, I see a lifetime of world-dust in a single dream.

Sent to Abbot Whole-Quiet

To the third peak north of Lone-Dragon Ridge, he fled back
home. He's grown old and lazy, his tumble-down house all

green-azure distances, a few roofbeams. It's a place so deep
among cold clouds you can't even hear temple bells calling.

Thinking of Golden-Tomb City Long Ago

1

Dragons-Radiant Monastery beneath Boat-Wreck Mountain,
Five-Dragon Pavilion beside Dark-Enigma Lake: it feels like

looking into ancient times here, wandering through all that
history-mist and cloud-blur, waters boundless and beyond.

2

History-mist and cloud-blur, waters boundless and beyond,
weed-tangled city walls wrap around ruins. Brush-choked

sight's a lifetime of world-dust lamenting all our struggles,
the past traced everywhere in thought, impossible to forget.

3

The past traced everywhere in thought, impossible to forget,
water reflects trees kingfisher-green and vines silvered azure.

Sublime monasteries survive, people say, but I'm content
to sail ravaged canals back into that inner pattern of things.

Parting in River-Serene

Ravaged chrysanthemums blacken. Autumn wind returns,
and rain like the rain when early plums ripen to yellow.

Hand in hand, why talk? We gaze together into grief every-
where in sight. Isn't this where mind knows itself utterly?

On a Farewell Journey to Send Off
Mend-Source, a Sudden Windstorm Rages,
So I Write Four Lines on the Boat's Wall

At the Huai River mouth, west wind turns
brutal. My friend's stuck here who knows

how long. But look: the rising moon turns
all these thoughts we share incandescent!

Climbing Up to Treasure-Master's Grave-Shrine

At pine gates, exhausted houseboy and horse refuse to go on.
I take my walking-stick of burl-gnarl bamboo, trust root-stone

and a river moon arcing into emptiness. It's bright as midday.
Mountain clouds drift shadow everywhere, dusk smoldering.

A racket of busy squirrels scatters among the silence of peaks.
Crows grow faint in outland cold, shadows looking into flight.

Here in the midst of all this, I can't tell who is guest, who host:
this old master's forgotten me utterly, and I've forgotten words.

Drifting South Creek

Drifting South Creek, I follow blossoms
away. Rowing home, it's a confusion of

scented dark. No idea where I am, I find
sun sinking away west of a painted bridge.

Again at South-Creek Tower, Written on a Wall

North Mountain clouds stretch on and on.
South Creek cascades all distances away.

Leaving my no-self vows behind, I climb
this tower again, exact everything in sight.

On a moonlit island bridge

On a moonlit island bridge, I think of mountain peaks, then
look down and mourn how water slips past. Who can know

distances? Tonight, I hear that sobbing from long ago again,
but gaze at a mountain moon and talk of this island bridge.

Written on Master Lake-Shadow's Wall

Thatch-eave paths are always well-swept, pure, free of moss,
and with your hands, flowering orchards planted themselves.

A creek meanders by, snug curve cradling jade-green fields,
as two mountains push a door open, send green-azure inside.

Napping at noon

Napping at noon, I lie beside blossoms on mats of streamwater
current. When sun turns shadow red, I raise blinds to look deep.

Seeing me, birds cry and startle away through this dream where
distant rivers and mountains hold sorrow's every twist and turn.

Written on a Wall at Balance-Peace Post-Station

Mountains seem sun-dyed clarity, warm
winds opening radiance across grasses.

As plums scatter a few flecks of snow,
wheat founders in a long river of cloud.

Spring Rain

Bitter mist hides spring colors. Grief-
drizzle sickens the splendor of things.

That dark isolate wonder impossible
now, I swill down a cup of dusk haze.

Looking at a Painting of Lumen Island

Lumen Island and its city walls revealed in this painting: they
remind me how I once moored a boat there at West Pavilion,

but heart and mind given to old age can't find long-ago times.
I rely on rivers and mountains for what's ancient and remains.

Above the Yangtze

River water churns, breathing west wind.
River blossoms scatter late reds. Drifting

longing's grief, flute-song carries through
haphazard eastern mountains and beyond.

Leaving the City

I've lived in the country long enough to know its wild joys:
it feels like I'm a child back home in my old village again.

Leaving the city today, I put all that gritty dust behind me,
and facing mountains and valleys, feel them enter my eyes.

After *Clouds Limitless* by a Monk at Nirvana-Radiant Monastery on Mist-Perch Mountain

In this isolate silence, distances beyond
human realms, there's no one to share

my joys. I sit at night, old age forgotten
completely, no need for purifying fasts.

No-mind is the Buddhist project. When-
ever guests wonder about this tradition,

I laugh, call it western wind's *ch'i*-mind,
perfectly empty and yet not empty at all.

There's a Huge Pine Beside the Road, and People Think It Promises Enlightenment

All gnarled dragon scales and whiskers no one could haul away,
it stands alone, ten thousand feet high, shading South Mountain.

Shouldn't we mourn how nowhere escapes the axe? So why use
pine-sap torch flames to brighten our struggle for enlightenment?

Sun west and low

Sun west and low: stair-shadow and churning kindred-trees.
Blinds raised: half-empty bamboo, green-azure mountains.

Ducks blurred in fire drift, gold on the chill of deep water,
dreams a ruins of distance and worry among this birdsong.

Off-Hand Poem

It's a blessing, the ten thousand things
spoken. Don't forget even a single line,

for I'm sending in these words a place
far from this loud world of confusion.

Spirit creatures

Spirit creatures ascending heaven—if you could train one,
you could ride along, but who can bridle such scaly majesty?

And they're far beyond trapping or killing, so how could
anyone know a dragon's *ch'i*-mind all boundless and wild?

Radiance-Hut

I understood Radiance-Hut Monastery today.
Ox-Head Mountain stands resolute at the gate,

but graves are tangled mulberry and bamboo,
terrace and temple a ruins of jade and gold.

A newborn calf sleeps in windblown silence.
Evening crows take flight one by one. Each

sight opens thousand-year dreams, no words
enough even for tonight's blossoms and rain.

Life at Samadhi-Forest Monastery

A stream winds around my home, mountain around bamboo:
mountain and stream always there, even among white cloud.

On a boat, gazing across this stream, I'm the mountain adrift.
It's an idleness stream birds and mountain wildflowers share.

Written on Eightfold-Integrity River

Wanting to search out *aranya* seclusion,
I drag my sandals over East Ridge to this

river valley. Wildflower beauty is rare
here, but mulberries reveal spring wind.

Farewell to Gaze-Arrive

Pond a scatter of emerald-green fields,
terrace a radiant riot of crimson bloom:

who can exhaust the splendor of spring?
There's no limit to mind's own delight.

With my goosefoot staff

With my goosefoot staff, I wander the stream winding around
East Ridge. When interest fades, I go home to bed. But in dream,

emperors Yao and Chieh sometimes appear: one noble, one vile.
So my practice isn't over. There are a few last things to forget.

Suddenly

Suddenly spring's ending. I close my brush-bramble gate,
green leaves already flooding the city, thick with shadow.

Old-age years are like this. I've lost the urge to see places,
but is there anywhere this spring wind can't go wandering?

Above the Yangtze

North of the Yangtze, autumn darkness spreads halfway open,
and evening clouds heavy with rain hang low across the land.

Wandering amid green-azure mountains, all roads lost, I see
a thousand sails suddenly come shimmering through shadow.

Wandering at Delight-Mind Pavilion, Sent to My Sister in Ch'ien-chou

Skies exquisite clearing over a thousand peaks
and ten thousand miles of rain-soaked autumn

clarity. Heaven's Star River cascading, flooding
down through an incandescent mirror of moon.

It rinses eye and spirit away, leaving only body
and shadow. Who wouldn't grieve in this far

end of darkness? Isolate mystery may deepen,
but I still long to see you wandering toward me.

Anchored on Abandon River

Creaking oars quicken. River sun
sinks into azure distances. There's

stillness in my wandering. Tides
drift east and west, day and night.

A Spring Day

I gaze into moss at my brushwood gate, rainwater radiant,
then wander through spring, blossoms crowding branches

everywhere. People travel distant roads and never arrive,
but all day here, birds in song leave and come back again.

Just to Say

I close my gate, wanting to end grief,
but grief won't go away. Then spring

wind comes, and I want to keep grief
close, but somehow grief won't stay.

After Elder-Ease's Poem *Buddha-Wind Ch'in*

The ten thousand things aren't quiet. There's always sound
happening. And there's no end to people's lament and song.

Once you know this, you know mind's no different. Trust it,
its sounds: they too are heaven's loom of origins unfurling.

Listening to Floodwater Past Midnight

Floodwater cascades ten thousand feet, rocky shorelines twisted,
and autumn sounds scatter away through sorrows of cloud past

midnight. On a moonlit island bridge, I listen to headlong water.
Bell Mountain: all night alone here, and it never leaves my mind.

On Tower Heights

I row among horizon swells, wander
uneasy on tower heights. No welcome

in flooding billows, how could my
oars reach those kindred distances?

Following Apricot-Blossom Rhymes

The season's wanton beauty: it startles the eye's gaze first,
then a plucked branch fills thoughts with a shy fragrance,

and a country girl tucks it into her hair. But it only brings
more shame over her grief-torn life of brushwood hairpins.

Spring Skies Clear

After ten days of early spring rain, rain
ends. Skies clear. I open my gate, gaze

clear into moss, content its azure-green
ripples won't come seeping into robes.

Sent to Abbot Whole-Repose

Bone-elegant, eyebrow-scruffy, you're done coming and going
among people. It's in occurrence appearing that they know your

clarity now. *Ch'i*-mind deep in idleness, you take up poem-brush
again; and beyond calm, you rival the serenity of Exalt Mountain.

Mornings, wanting to move like clouds, you turn visitors away,
and nights invite the river moon to gaze out over frontier passes.

All trace of me keeps swirling away in this world of dust. It's sad,
such loss, but it means I'm majestic as any lone peak I might face.

A Country Walk

They've picked mulberry leaves clean. Green shade's scarce,
now silkworms have spun fat cocoons in grass-weave racks.

I want to stop at a village house and ask about local customs,
how it is such bitter work could earn such miserable hunger.

Pure-Apparent Monastery

Pure-Apparent, ancient monastery
twenty autumns deserted and cold:

it's seen the ruin ravaging kalpas,
and now I come cultivating origins.

Cricket Weaving-Song

The gold screens and kingfisher-green curtains of autumn.
Returning year after year, too drunk to understand, crickets

face threadbare houses, song spurring loom-shuttles on.
How many houses here own even a single thread of silk?

On this side, flood-strewn

On this side, flood-strewn streams vein these mountains,
and the other side's buried in cloud, no mountains to see.

Rain has come, but why plow water margins? Setting out
wearing robes of cloud, we can sleep in mountain depths.

Ninth Month, *Yi* Year of the Snake, On Climbing Metal-Forge Wall

I need this view of Bell Mountain Peak,
so I often take the path to Metal-Forge,

scrambling up out of shadowy treetops,
thinking of places I wandered long ago.

A sun drowned in red rises over islands,
thornwood mist silver-azure. So much

loss and wounded lament, but ancient
river and mountain remain unchanged.

River Rain

All dark and distant mystery, river rain soaks yellow twilight.
Heavens enter recluse islands, brimful, misting them together,

and North Creek pours through South Creek waters. Suddenly,
South Mountain's meandering around North Mountain clouds.

Written on a Wall at Source-Aware Monastery's Bamboo-Dragon Terrace

The words in this northern terrace's name are such enduring
masters. I write them into a poem of reverence, where river

wind and mountain rain come sweeping through, seething,
and suddenly, wild dragons among delicate bamboo cry out.

At Broken-Tomb Shores

1

Remnant gravestones sunk and buried in springtime grasses,
winds over and over spirit up whirls of dust across the land.

Past midnight, pearl and jade lay scattered on gravemounds,
and somehow people still need to beg for the least offerings.

2

Remnant coffins will poke out how many springs from now,
and tangled weeds in desolate winds will bury magic horses.

It isn't like long ago, gravemound guests drunk and well-fed:
now they come gathering sticks and dry grass for their fires.

Farewell to Candor-Achieve

Traveling north we delight in family,
and drifting south savor friends. How

could we forget each other? We gaze
anywhere into all our kindred depths.

Winter-Solstice Sacrifice

Bright stars are sad and tired. Moon is a ragged confusion.
Earth's ten thousand holes fill with wind and start grieving.

People scatter through temple gates. Lamp flames go dark.
Most of the time, we're alone searching remnants of dream.

The Ancient Pine

Through layer after thick layer, its trunk rises a thousand feet,
towering up into azure skies, nothing to do with forests below.

Winds from ten thousand valleys crowding it with night sounds,
thousand-mountain moonlight haunting it with autumn shadow,

it's rooted deep in Change-Maker's vast heaven-and-earth mind.
How could tending it with rich soil ever strengthen such power?

Needing timber for fine terraces and temples, people dream of it,
but no woodworker's skilled enough, so it lives on free of harm.

Late Spring

There's no limit to remnant reds clothing earth in their scatter,
and on canyon heights, cloud clings to kingfisher-green trees.

Only these poplar blossoms understand the wind's *ch'i*-mind:
chasing each other away into clear blue skies never to return.

In Jest, Sent to Abbot Empty-White

White cloud on mountain summits, my *ch'an* friend grows sick.
We were renowned luminaries once, sent poems to each other,

but journeys vanish into four directions, lives into eighty years.
We return to a wildland temple, and who understands us then?

At Dragon-Spring Monastery's Stone Well

1

For a thousand years, the mountain's stone flank has grown
sleek. Its rocky eye is a dry spring of Absence. Everything

alive in all beneath heaven is waiting for rain. Dragon still
here: who knows it gazing out at its rippled twists and curls?

2

People say this pond has never gone dry. Now there's ash-
green wool tangled across the bottom, a confusion of moss.

There's drought everywhere within the four seas, rain rare,
and the reason's here too: dragon all Absence sound asleep.

At the Shrine-Hut on Eightfold-Integrity River

Alone in recluse quiet can be enough,
reality absolute itself such clear joy,

and mountains never hold eyes back,
river sounds never grate against ears.

Suddenly, there's nothing at all to be.
What I am now I am, and am, and am.

Wandering Bell Mountain

Two peaks all pine and oak and shadowy red vines, a stream
at the heart of it all: it's perfect as Peach-Blossom paradise.

From noon chants in cloud, I know there's a monastery near,
but return home in dusk light without visiting monk friends.

Autumn Wind

Gathering and keeping is an arrogant greed.
Heaven's loom of origins works its own way.

Where the wall curves, a faint rustle begins,
then a full racket kicks up beside the house

and the countryside startles into sandstorm
as confusions of willow treetops break apart.

How can river and lake be inside these eyes?
Last night I dreamed wild billows and swells.

Farewell at the River Tower

This clear stream keeps leaving these hundred mountains rising
ridge beyond ridge, and you're a windblown thing carried north.

Past midnight, my thoughts at ease where shadowy origins of it
all begin, a moon lights this lone form I am, friend to cold pines.

Bell Mountain

Oaring north, sailing south, we anchor among the world's four
boundaries. The mountain's gold confusion of emerald green

beguiles us, its single root spreading a hundred thousand feet
beneath waves and swells all flood-dragons people never know.

Meeting an Old Friend at Splendor-Hoard Monastery

A hundred worries close mind's depths,
but in a single laugh they open and stay.

Wandering west wind outside city walls,
we watch orchards scatter their lit colors

ablaze, seeing perception is like a dream.
Who could bear brimmed wine too? Joy

falters, but we can set out again through
rivers and lakes spread boundlessly away.

A Moonlit Night in Mid-Autumn, Sent to Broad-Origin and My Other Brothers

Drifting clouds along quiet as tufts of autumn feather,
igniting gold ripples in a glass of stale wine, it's come

thousands of miles to test my poetry skills. But in this
altar of night, who could match the elegance of wind?

South of Town, Leaving

A north wind startles across these Manifest-Ease river waters,
and the boat sets out, cuts full-sail through boundless swells.

Mile after mile, our eyes offer Household Mountain farewell,
a thousand years of empty hopes in the drift of cicada song.

This Spirit-Vulture Mountain

This Spirit-Vulture Mountain—how could it be our enemy?
People come, relentless axe and blade hacking, haul its jade-

pure water-crystal off to market. Then the din of haggling:
all those market people making enemies of each other too.

Farewell to a Monk Leaving
for Heaven-Terrace Mountain

Heaven-Terrace is a hundred sixty thousand feet high, and the year
ending, but you set out for home, an old monk with his walking-stick.

The road passes through such majesty. How could chants explain it:
traces of kingfisher green lost in snow-mist and confusions of cloud?

Parting in River-Serene

Gazing at each other, we're held here.
Dusk lake tranquil, we sit hand in hand,

talk fallen silent. Slow, deep in radiant
moonlight, island after island emerges.

Following Prosper Bright-Gather's Rhymes

Lost to my country, I'm living on Bell Mountain. Green pines,
courtyard walls, rooms: the monastery's hidden among sunlit

mist. Here, sound itself reveals Buddha-nature perfectly: this
wind whispering then wailing, streams hushed then tumbling.

Following the Rhymes of Abbot Elder-Guide's Poem *The Sound of Majestic Pines*

Indifferent to our human heart, heaven's loom of origins stirs.
It opens among us this sound from beyond things themselves,

this dark clamor filling these rooms. No guest could dream it,
and at dawn, grieving on a thousand peaks, it startles gibbons

awake. In the shrine, it whispers three depths on a sad *ch'in*,
and outside this room, its wind-chant laments everything lost.

Old songs of passion bewilder simple ears. But once you start
listening to this loom of sound, it returns mind to such clarity.

Thoughts on Bell Mountain

Incense and candles draw me to this mountain. Empty mind
graced by old age here, clappers sound night's slow hours.

And this ridgetop wandering, heart-stricken and confused:
tomorrow it will be spring wind coming and going of itself.

Plum Blossoms Along the Canal

Sun warming my back, I linger on and on along the canal,
cherishing fragrant depths in this season of sunlit snow.

Who needs a friend when evening dark comes? I'll come
again here by moonlight, gaze into confusions of shadow.

Skies Clearing

Before dawn clouds smolder a pale smear of blackest red,
I watch snowflakes in runnels between rooftiles steaming.

Mountains keep waiting to scatter free into bright morning
cold: two or three peaks caught deep here in white cloud.

Hair white

Hair white, delusions over but taken by still more sickness,
I drag my bed out and sleep among bamboo, facing autumn

darkness. Morning comes. Geese drift, backs to a west-wind
gale rinsing this ten-thousand-mile river-and-lake mind away.

Thoughts Sent on My Way Home from River-Serene, After Stopping to Gaze at Samadhi-Forest Monastery

My lame donkey hates the stony road
up there, and I'm done with big climbs.

It seems forever since I saw you, my old
monk friend. Our youth suddenly gone,

I keep following morning clouds away,
then race evening birds back into this

valley of pines all shadowed dark. Here,
I know you in the distances between us.

Following the Rhymes of a Poem
Sent by Encompass-Anew

Inexhaustible *ch'i*-mind of high mountains and flowing rivers
fill a stringless *ch'in* in my lap, its three feet of empty music.

Who can understand this silence so perfectly dark and deep?
Sitting here beside a river tower, I watch geese rise into flight.

A Friend in Mourning Visits River-Serene

Who ever lives out life's full hundred years? It's the body's
grief. And gazing through spring wind, your eyes weep tears.

Birds in song, open blossoms—everything has its thoughts.
Don't forget the poetry in mountain cherry and pied wagtail.

Recognizing Myself

Shores cold, bamboo leans and sways.
Water clear, chestnuts ripple and swell

as shrimp stir, waving whiskers adrift,
and fish rouse, frolic fins and flappers.

I put down my walking-stick and rest,
then lifting my robe, cross the stream,

recognizing myself carefree on a whim,
a butterfly fluttering on through dream.

The Ancient Monastery

Halfway into ruins, this isolate monastery is wind-scoured
silence I wander all year, ritual shoes frayed and tattered.

In the meditation hall, where a last few roofbeams remain,
dust golden at dusk falls across sutra-stones like dusk rain.

Sent to the Painter, Sage-Cloud, in River-Serene

Seeing yourself all ruins of age, it's easy to guess the truth.
Sage-Cloud's brush may conjure the spirit of some real me,

but when I try to leave Bell Mountain, I can't tear myself
loose. If I did, it would scatter this not-yet-dead self away.

Summer Night on a Boat, Chill in the Air

My frail body afraid even of morning heat,
I trust to boat-masts and the coming night:

late sun drifting away with clouds of flame,
wind and water-mist turning cold. Autumn

hasn't come feathering sick bones into air,
and last light is rinsing tangled dread away,

leaving my river-and-lake *ch'i*-mind strong
again, surging on and on and nothing lost.

On mountain slopes

On mountain slopes, farmers in courtyards offer seeds to gods.
Outside city walls, people hang lanterns on terraces and towers.

But facing spring with so much white hair, I just sleep and sleep,
and when a bird sings through that sleep, I'm sick of it all again.

At the Mouth of Lumen River

West of Lumen City, a hundred mountains rise ridge beyond ridge.
All trace of my life buried in these dark depths of haze and cloud,

it's perfectly empty: that worry over white hair, over all I've done
and not done. In spring wind, the river lights up this ravaged face.

Drifting Grain-Thresh River

To ease illness and the ruins of age, I sail river currents.
Spring wind scares me, and the noon-tide; but I'm new

now, a person sharing *ch'i*-mind with wild blossoms, so
is there anywhere mountains won't welcome me home?

Old now, tangled

Old now, tangled in human form, I'm done trusting wisdom.
Knowledge in ruins, I'll follow farmland elders, live out my

hundred years like a child. What else could carry me clear
through, heal all these failures hacking and scarring my face?

Written on a Wall at
Half-Mountain Monastery

1

When I wander, heaven starts raining,
and when I stop, rain sets out for home.

How could rain be my own wandering?
Meeting here was that carefree and easy.

2

If it's cold, I just settle somewhere warm,
and if it's hot, I wander somewhere cool:

all beings here no different from Buddha,
Buddha precisely all beings themselves.

Poking Fun at My White Hair

Long since afraid of tumbling like windblown thistledown
away, you hide in your cap, never dare leave. Spring wind

scatters you away, but never lasts long. And even thin, you
flare incandescent beneath bright moon and stars and stars.

White Hair's Answer

Old age brings white hair. Heaven's loom of origins works
like that. People never denounce summer's endless green:

they love spring blossoms and those long days that follow.
But soon autumn leaves fall, and did ancients outlive that?

Above the River

1

Tide swells vast across windblown waters.
Sand stretches away. We sit, lingering out

all this clarity a setting sun deepens across
empty river expanses. Not a single boat out

anywhere, we see reed-thatch huts, people
struggling at their hopes for millet and rice.

They never lament such hard-earned food.
It's ugly this year for half our nine regions.

2

A letter from river shores arrives, describing
villages tangled thick in sickness and hunger.

Why are they telling me, a ten-thousand-mile
wanderer, swelling my hundred-year sorrow?

No one cares about patching up ruined lives
now, and my lifework's only turned to shame.

My sick eyes gaze off southwest. Night falls.
I trust myself to this little-boat life cast adrift.

On the Terrace, for Mind-Source

Grown old, I can't read tiny script,
but bamboo mats offer comforting

darkness of sleep. Taking it, words
deserted, I'm almost newborn again!

Gazing North

Hair whiter still, I ache to see those long-ago northlands,
but keep to this refuge: goosefoot staff, windblown trees.

Pity the new moon: all that bright beauty, and for whom?
It's dusk. Countless mountains face each other in sorrow.

I can't see anything of this autumn day

I can't see anything of this autumn day,
its last few scraps of yellow in treetops.

Out with my goosefoot staff, I think of
serene fields, but looking find no light.

It scares me. From streams and valleys,
icy winds blow through jacket and robe,

and a beautiful empty-mountain moon
means frost covering my cap is radiant.

Reading History

Renowned achievement's been bitter business from the beginning.
Who can you trust to tell the story of all you've done and not done?

Whatever happens is already murky enough, and full of distortion,
then small minds muddle the truth further, and it's utter confusion.

They only hand down dregs. Their green-azure and cinnabar inks
can't capture that fresh kernel of things, that quintessential spirit,

and how could they fathom a lofty sage's *ch'i*-mind, those witless
sentinels guarding thousand-autumn dust on their pages of paper?

Chants

1

Work failing, I'm shamed by my image in water, and now
world-dust fills my eyes again, it's grief to see mountains.

Smoke and haze all boundless silence south of the river:
there isn't much keeping me here among people's houses.

3

Dawn lights up the room. I close my book and sleep,
dreaming of Bell Mountain and full of tenderness.

How do you grow old living with failure and disgrace?
Stay close to the cascading creek: cold, shimmering.

Thoughts as I Lie Alone

Alone, a noon dove calling in spring
shade, I lie in a valley of forest quiet.

Scraps of cloud pass, scattering rain,
and I listen, late in life, to its clatter.

Eyes full of red and green confusion,
our sad times unraveling my legacy,

there's no word near these thoughts
still as Bell Mountain in its slumber.

Cut Flowers

Getting this old isn't much fun,
and it's worse stuck in bed, sick.

I draw water and arrange flowers,
comforted by their scents adrift,

scents adrift, gone in a moment.
And how much longer for me?

Cut flowers and this long-ago I:
it's so easy forgetting each other.

Notes

Relatively few of Wang An-shih's late poems can be dated with assurance. Two periods for which biographical details appear in the poems are the primary exception to this: the months following Wang's resignation as Prime Minister, during which he begins his quiet life as a Ch'an poet, and the years just before his death, when he faced old age and the failure of his reforms. These two groups of poems naturally appear at the beginning and end of this book. Otherwise, the arrangement is not meant to imply a chronology for the poems, and no doubt a few date from before Wang's late years.

3   **mind:** In ancient China, there was no fundamental distinction between heart and mind: the term (心) connotes all that we think of in the two concepts together, though the mental dimension of this concept usually refers not to the analytical faculty as in the West, but to empty consciousness itself. In the Ch'an Buddhist conceptual framework within which Wang An-shih's poetry operates, 心 very often refers only to empty consciousness and is virtually synonymous with two other common Ch'an terms: *empty mind* and *no-mind* (see below).
    idle: Idleness is a kind of meditative wandering in which you move with the effortless spontaneity of Tao (see Introduction, p. xiv), a state in which daily life becomes the essence of spiritual practice. Etymologically, the ideogram for *idleness* connotes "profound serenity and quietness," its pictographic elements rendering a tree standing alone within the gates to a courtyard, or, in its alternate form, a moon shining through open gates: 閑 (閒).

4   *ch'an* **stillness:** *Ch'an* is the Chinese translation of *dhyana*, Sanskrit for "sitting meditation." The Ch'an (Japanese: Zen) Buddhist sect takes that name because it focuses so resolutely on sitting meditation. See Introduction, especially p. xvi.

5   **Samadhi-Forest Monastery:** Located on Bell Mountain, this is the monastery Wang An-shih adopted as a second home after leaving his position as Prime Minister and moving to River-Serene in the southeast. He lived at Samadhi-Forest for the first months after his arrival there, and then returned often in the years that followed, as

it was only a short walk from his house. It therefore appears often in Wang's poems.

Samadhi: A meditative state of undifferentiated awareness in which there is no distinction between subject and object.

7 **master of Tao:** Ch'an Buddhism was a homegrown amalgam of philosophical Taoism and imported Buddhism, so a "master of Tao" was in a sense both a Ch'an master and a master of Lao Tzu's philosophical system.

empty: This recurring concept resonates in a number of Taoist and Buddhist ways. In general it is essentially synonymous with Absence (see Introduction, p. xiii). As such it is often used to describe mind itself—consciousness emptied of all content. When used in reference to the empirical world, it suggests that the ten thousand things are empty in the sense that they are exactly what they are, free of any imposed constructions of the human mind. And perhaps more fundamentally, they are also spoken of as empty because they are fleeting forms that are most essentially the generative tissue of Absence (emptiness) itself.

8 **Bright-Distance:** Dissatisfied with his rule, the legendary Yellow Emperor (regnant 2698–2598 B.C.E.) dreamt of a social paradise called Bright-Distance. He took it as a model for his rule, and soon transformed China into a similarly perfect society. The name also refers to the place where people first appeared just after primal emptiness separated into heaven and earth.

Absence: The generative tissue from which the ten thousand things arise. See Introduction, p. xiii.

9 **no-mind:** Consciousness emptied of all contents, a state reached through deep *ch'an* meditation. Also called "empty mind." See Introduction, p. xvi.

11 **tides:** The ocean tides flow back up into the Yangtze river as far as the region where Wang An-shih lived.

13 **River-Serene:** The city (present-day Nanjing) near which Wang An-shih lived. See Introduction, p. xix.

East Ridge: A ridge on Bell Mountain that appears often in Wang's poems.

Star River: The Milky Way.

Earth's ten thousand holes . . . : From *Chuang Tzu* 2.1:

"This Mighty Mudball of a world spews out breath, and that breath is called wind," began Adept Piebald. "Everything is fine so long as it's still. But when it blows, the ten thousand holes cry and moan. Haven't you heard them wailing on and on? In the awesome beauty of mountain forests, it's all huge trees a hundred feet around, and they're full of wailing hollows and holes like noses, like mouths, like ears, like posts and beams, like cups and bowls, like empty ditches and puddles: water-splashers, arrow-whistlers, howlers, gaspers, callers, screamers, laughers, warblers—leaders singing out *yuuu!* and followers answering *yeee!* When the wind's light, the harmony's gentle; but when the storm wails, it's a mighty chorus. And then, once the fierce wind has passed through, the holes are all empty again. Haven't you seen felicity and depravity thrashing and flailing together?"

"So the music of earth means all those holes singing together," said Adept Adrift, "and the music of humans means bamboo pipes singing. Could I ask you to explain the music of heaven for me?"

"Sounding the ten thousand things differently, so each becomes itself according to itself alone—what could make such music?"

14 **clouds . . . source:** It was popularly believed that clouds were born among high mountain slopes and valleys, because scraps of cloud often appear to be rising from there into the sky.

15 ***ch'in***: A very ancient stringed instrument revered by Chinese intellectuals as a means for attaining enlightenment, the *ch'in* often appears in poems and was used as accompaniment when Chinese poets chanted their verse. Here it is a metaphor for the poet himself. In the hands of a master, a *ch'in* could voice with profound clarity the rivers-and-mountains realm, no-mind, even the very source of all things. Hence, it could speak at depths beyond words. And so, even more profound than a *ch'in* played is an "unplayed" *ch'in* (here) or a "stringless" *ch'in* (p. 73).

Presence and Absence: See Introduction, p. xiii.

17 **heaven:** A recurring concept that historically referred to an impersonal divine power controlling the cosmos. With the rise of Taoist philosophy

(c. sixth century B.C.E.), in which the physical Cosmos is conceived as a self-generating organic whole, *heaven* came to mean something like "natural process." Here, it is hardly distinguishable from Tao. Heaven also combines with earth in the formulation "heaven and earth," which refers to the two fundamental elements of the Cosmos, heaven being the *yang* and earth the *yin*. And through it all, heaven retained its original meaning, which was simply "sky."

dragon: Another recurring concept, the dragon was China's mythological embodiment of the awesome force of change, of life itself; and so it was both feared and revered. Legend describes the seasons in terms of the dragon's movements: Small as a silkworm and vast as all heaven and earth, the dragon descends into deep waters in autumn, where it hibernates until spring, when its reawakening means the return of life to earth. It rises and ascends into the sky, where it billows into thunderclouds and falls as spring's life-bringing rains. Its claws flash as lightning in those thunderclouds, and its rippling scales glisten in the bark of rain-soaked pines.

sweeping my gate-path clean: A traditional gesture of welcome for anticipated visitors.

18 **Kindred-Tree:** The *ch'in* (see note to p. 15) was made from the wood of kindred-trees, which gave the trees a certain spiritual aura. The standard English name is "parasol tree," and it is in the chocolate family.

empty-mind: Consciousness emptied of all contents, a state reached through deep *ch'an* meditation. See Introduction p. xiv.

yang . . . yin: The two fundamental forces of the universe: male and female, hot and cold, light and dark, heaven and earth. They arose from an undifferentiated primordial unity, and their interaction gives birth perennially to the empirical universe, its ten thousand things, and their constant transformations.

21 **Integrity:** *Te* from the title *Tao Te Ching*, which literally means "The Classic of the Tao and Integrity (to Tao)."

23 **dream:** This story, known as the Yellow-Millet Dream, recounts how a sage named Lu Sheng stopped to rest at a house while traveling. There, as the master of the house cooked millet for the guest, a poor servant-boy complained bitterly about the difficulty of his life. At Lu Sheng's suggestion, the boy lay down and dreamt of an alternate life in which he marries a beautiful woman, becomes Prime Minister,

and lives to the age of eighty. When the boy woke, he had lived an entire life, but the millet had not yet finished cooking.

25 **loom of origins:** A mythic image for the deep structure from which is woven the constantly evolving fabric of the Cosmos. According to Chuang Tzu: "The ten thousand things all emerge from a loom of origins, and they all vanish back into it." See also pp. 25, 49, 63, 69, 80.

26 **Golden-Tomb:** Ancient name for River-Serene, the city near which Wang An-shih lived. With a population of over a million people, Golden-Tomb was perhaps the largest city in the world when it was razed in 589 by a military campaign that reunified China and led to the T'ang Dynasty. Although rebuilt, the city was much smaller than before, and many ruins remained. Several centuries before Wang An-shih, the great T'ang poet Li Po also wrote about the city's ruins:

At Golden-Tomb

Golden-Tomb City tucked into the earth,
the river curving past, flowing away:

there were once a million homes here,
and crimson towers along narrow lanes.

A vanished country all spring grasses,
the palace buried in ancient hills, this

moon remains, facing timeless islands
across Thereafter Lake waters, empty.

ch'i: *Ch'i* is often described as the universal breath-force; but understood more fully, it is a continuous generative source, the matter and energy of the Cosmos seen together as a single breath-force surging though its perpetual transformations.

ch'i-mind: This recurring term (意) is generally translated as "thought," or "intention." It can refer to an individual's "thought" or "intention," but it is just as often ascribed to the nonhuman world. There, it refers to the urge that generates the burgeoning-forth of things, each according to the dictates of its 意. Each particular thing, at its very origin, has its own 意, as does the Cosmos as a whole. This links human intention/thought to the originary movements of the Cosmos. And that link explains this translation's use of the term *"ch'i,"* for 意 can be described as the "intentionality" shaping the creative force of *ch'i*, which human consciousness shares with the fertile earth and indeed the entire Cosmos. See also pp. 40, 42, 52, 60, 73, 76, 78, 85.

30 **dust:** An oft-used metaphor for insubstantial worldly affairs.

31 **Dark-Enigma:** Tao before it is named and therefore reduced to human conception, before concepts like Absence and Presence (see Introduction, p. xiii.) give birth to each other: and so, that region where consciousness and Cosmos share their source. See also the *Tao Te Ching* poem on p. xiv–xv.

32 **inner pattern:** The philosophical meaning of *inner pattern* (理), which originally referred to the veins and markings in a precious piece of jade, is something akin to what we call natural law. It is the system of principles or patterns that governs the burgeoning-forth of Presence, the ten-thousand things, out of Absence.

34 **Treasure-Master:** An illustrious monk from the sixth century.
guest . . . host: Here, in a literal sense, Treasure-Master is the host, as it is his grave-shrine, and Wang An-shih is the guest. But this is enriched by two Ch'an uses of the terms: first, host as teacher, and guest as student; and second, host as one's original nature or empty consciousness, and guest as one's everyday mind with its thoughts and memories.

36 **planted themselves:** That is, the Master planted the orchard with such an empty mind that he was not distinguished from the orchard, so the "orchards planted themselves."

40 **Nirvana:** In Ch'an Buddhism, nirvana is not a transcendental state beyond the suffering of this world. Rather, it is a state of enlightenment very much of this world, a state in which consciousness is emptied of all content and self is identified with the emptiness (Absence) that is the true nature of all things.
western wind: In the most profound reading, this "western wind" is simply western wind. But there's a secondary allusion to Buddhism,

which came to China from India in the west. In particular, legend says that Ch'an was brought to China from the west by Boddhidharma. Interestingly, to say Buddhism has *ch'i*-mind is to say that it shares its source and nature with the generative process of the Cosmos.

41 **South Mountain:** Calling up such passages as "like the timelessness of South Mountain" in *The Book of Songs* (*Shih Ching*, 166.6), South Mountain came to possess a kind of mythic stature as the embodiment of the elemental and timeless nature of the earth.

44 **aranya:** Sanskrit term for a forest hermitage suited to quiet meditation.

45 **Yao and Chieh:** Yao was a mythic emperor (regnant 2356–2255 B.C.E.) of great sagacity who ruled during the legendary golden age of China. Chieh, by contrast, was the tyrannical final emperor of the Hsia Dynasty (regnant 1818–1766 B.C.E.). His infamous depravity led to the collapse of the dynasty.

47 **spirit:** *Spirit* (魂) was not conceived among ancient Chinese artist-intellectuals as the immortal soul of the West. Instead, it was considered a condensation of *ch'i* energy that dissolves back into the overall movement of *ch'i* at death.

51 **azure-green...seeping into robes:** A play on this poem by the great T'ang Dynasty poet Wang Wei (701–761 C.E.):

The Way It Is

Faint shadow, a house, and traces of rain.
In courtyard depths, the gate's still closed

past noon. That lazy, I gaze at moss until
its green-azure comes seeping into robes.

52 **occurrence appearing:** A central concept in Taoist cosmology, *tzu-jan* is a way of describing the process of Tao (see Introduction, p. xiv f.) that emphasizes individual entities rather than the process as a whole. Its literal meaning is "self-so" or "the of-itself," which as a philo-sophical concept becomes "being such of itself," hence "spontaneous" or "natural." But a more revealing translation of *tzu-jan* is "occurrence appearing of itself," for the term is meant to describe the ten thousand

things burgeoning forth spontaneously from the generative source, each according to its own nature, independent and self-sufficient, each dying and returning to the process of change, only to reappear in another self-generating form.

53 **kalpa:** A cosmic cycle extending from the creation of a world-system to its destruction—traditionally given as 4,320,000 years.

54 **Cricket Weaving-Song:** Silk was produced and woven in poor farm villages. It was thought that cricket song sounded like the whirr of looms, and that in autumn their song was encouraging the women in their loom work.

58 **Earth's ten thousand holes:** See note to p. 13.

59 **Ancient Pine:** This poem's little fable echoes a number of tales in the *Chuang Tzu*: 1.16 and 4.4, for instance, or this from 4.5:

> When Adept Piebald was wandering in the Shang hills, he came across a tree unlike any other. It was so huge it could shelter a thousand teams of horses in its shade.
>
> "What kind of tree is this?" wondered Adept Piebald. "It's timber must be of the rarest and most treasured kind." But looking up, he saw that its spindly branches were too twisted for beams and its massive trunk was too gnarled and mealy for coffins. He tasted a leaf, and it left his mouth burned and blistered. He sniffed, and the smell was bad enough to put someone into a crazed stupor for half a week.
>
> "So this tree's useless after all," he said. "No wonder it's so huge. Yes, yes—that's how it is for the sacred: they too have mastered uselessness."

Change-Maker: Tao.

heaven-and-earth: The two fundamental principles *yang and yin* at the cosmological scale. Hence, the Cosmos.

62 **Peach-Blossom paradise:** A utopian village found by travelers in T'ao Ch'ien's "Peach-Blossom Spring."

67 **Spirit-Vulture Mountain:** Named after a favorite retreat of the Buddha's. According to tradition, he handed down several major sutras there.

Heaven-Terrace Mountain: According to one legend, the mountain was the back of a vast turtle swimming in the ocean at the beginning of the world. At that time the sky had collapsed and the first-woman Lady She-Voice (Nu Kua) cut off the turtle's legs and used them as supports to hold the sky up. Then she moved the mountain to dry land so it would not sink into the ocean.

70 **empty mind:** Here, literally "host," from the Ch'an distinction between "host," meaning one's original nature or empty consciousness, and "guest," meaning one's everyday self (see note to p. 34).

73 **stringless *ch'in*:** See note to p. 15.

74 **recognizing myself . . . dream:** Echoing the famous butterfly story by Chuang Tzu (2.24), the seminal Taoist sage (the italicized phrase is quoted directly):

> Long ago, a certain Chuang Tzu dreamt he was a butterfly— a butterfly fluttering here and there, *recognizing itself carefree on a whim*, knowing nothing of Chuang Tzu. Then all of a sudden he woke to find that he was, beyond all doubt, Chuang Tzu. Who knows if it was Chuang Tzu dreaming a butterfly, or a butterfly dreaming Chuang Tzu? Chuang Tzu and butterfly: clearly there's a difference. This is called the transformation of things.

75 **sutra-stones:** Large upright slabs of stone (stelae) with sutras carved into them.

78 **tide:** See note to p. 11.

79 **Half-Mountain Monastery:** At the end of his life, Wang An-shih gave his house to the Ch'an community for use as a monastery (see Introduction, p. xxi), and he moved to a house in River-Serene. Here, he is visiting his former home in its new incarnation.

82 **my lifework's only turned to shame:** This and several of the following poems from very late in Wang's life lament the fact that the reforms he instituted as Prime Minister were being dismantled. See Introduction, p. xxi–xxii.

85 **History:** See Introduction, p. xxii.

Finding List

1. 臨川集 (Lin-ch'uan Chi). SPPY. (Chüan, page number, leaf, poem number).
2. 王荊文公詩箋註 (Wang Ching-wen Kung Shi Chien Chu). 李壁 (Li Pi), comm. (Page number with chüan number in parentheses). Page number is for the 1958 Beijing edition (Zhong-hua). Different editions of the Li Pi text have different page numbers, but the chüan number stays the same.

Page	1. *Lin-ch'uan Chi.*	2. *Wang Ching-wen Kung Shi Chien Chu.*
3	28.8b-2	562 (42)
	34.5b-4	675 (48)
4	28.3a-4	548 (42)
	33.7b-2	660 (47)
5	31.4a-3	612 (45)
	3.2a-3	37 (4)
6	23.4b-3	440 (35)
7	29.5a-2	573 (43)
	30.10a-1	607 (44)
8	29.3b-4	569 (43)
	26.3b-1	508 (40)
9	3.3a-3	39 (4)
10	14.4a-3.1	244 (22)

11	27.5b-4	535 (41)
	30.5a-1	592 (44)
12	28.9b-4	565 (42)
	27.6a-4	536 (41)
13	30.3a-1.3	588 (44)
	27.4a-1	531 (41)
14	1.7b-1	16 (2)
15	26.4a-5	509 (40)
	33.9a-5	665 (47)
16	29.4a-3	571 (43)
	26.4b-1	510 (40)
17	28.8a-1	560 (42)
	27.6a-3	536 (41)
18	16.5a-3	283 (25)
19	28.9a-2	563 (42)
	26.4a-7	510 (40)
20	27.7b-3	540 (41)
	28.9b-5	565 (42)
21	3.7a-2	48 (4)
	28.9b-2	564 (42)
22	14.7a-4	253 (22)
23	28.10a-1	565 (42)
	26.6b-3	517 (40)
24	29.5a-1	573 (43)
	29.5a-3	573 (43)

25	25.3a-1	487 (38)
26	30.3b-4	590 (44)
	26.5a-1	511 (40)
27	29.6a-1	575 (43)
	29.6a-3	576 (43)
28	16.3b-4	278 (24)
29	26.5a-3	512 (40)
	29.7a-1.1	579 (43)
30	29.7b-2	580 (43)
	34.10a-3	686 (48)
31	29.8a-2	582 (43)
33	29.8b-1	583 (43)
	26.5a-6	513 (40)
34	17.6b-2	312 (27)
35	26.5b-2	513 (40)
	26.5b-1	513 (40)
36	30.4a-2	590 (44)
	29.5a-4	574 (43)
37	30.4a-1	590 (44)
	26.4a-4	509 (40)
38	26.5b-6	514 (40)
	30.4a-3	590 (44)
39	26.5b-5	514 (40)
	31.7b-2	619 (45)

40	15.5a-3	263 (23)
41	30.6b-4	598 (44)
	30.5b-4	594 (44)
42	3.3a-2	39 (4)
	30.7b-3	601 (44)
43	14.7a-2	252 (22)
44	30.9b-3	606 (44)
	26.7a-1	517 (40)
45	26.8b-3	523 (40)
	27.5a-4	534 (41)
46	27.5a-3	534 (41)
	30.8b-2	603 (44)
47	15.6a-2	267 (24)
48	26.7a-5	518 (40)
	31.7a-4	618 (45)
49	3.5b-1	46 (4)
	31.9a-3.3	623 (45)
50	31.10b-3	627 (45)
	26.7a-6	519 (40)
51	32.2b-1.3	629 (46)
	26.7b-1	519 (40)
52	25.2b-2	486 (38)
53	32.5a-2	634 (46)
	26.7b-2	519 (40)

54	32.9b-2	646 (46)
	32.6a-3	63 (5)
55	10.3b-2	157 (14)
56	32.6a-4	637 (46)
	32.5b-3.1	636 (46)
57	32.5a-3	634 (46)
58	26.8b-2	522 (40)
	32.9b-3	646 (46)
59	23.8a-1	448 (35)
60	33.4a-1	651 (47)
	33.9a-2	664 (47)
61	33.5b-1	655 (47)
62	3.2b-2	38 (4)
	33.5a-2	654 (47)
63	14.8a-3	256 (23)
64	33.5b-3	656 (47)
	33.4b-5.1	653 (47)
65	14.8a-1	256 (23)
66	34.3b-3	669 (47)
	34.5a-4	673 (48)
67	34.3b-4	670 (48)
	34.4b-1	671 (48)
68		525 (40)
	27.9a-1	543 (41)

69	23.8a-3	449 (35)
70	28.5a-3	553 (42)
	28.6b-1	556 (42)
71	34.5a-2	673 (48)
	31.6b-2.1	596 (44)
72	14.6b-1	250 (22)
73	34.6a-3.1	676 (48)
	34.6b-1	676 (48)
74	3.6a-1	46 (4)
75	34.7a-3	679 (48)
	29.9a-5	585 (43)
76	16.5a-2	283 (25)
77	28.4b-2	552 (42)
	33.4a-3	652 (47)
78	29.9a-2	584 (43)
	27.5b-2	535 (41)
79	3.2a-1	36 (4)
80	27.7a-2	539 (41)
	27.7a-3	539 (41)
81	16.5a-1	281 (24)
83	26.4a-6	510 (40)
	33.9b-1	665 (47)
84	8.5a-1	129 (11)

85	25.7a-2	500 (39)
86	32.4a-3	632 (46)
87	3.6b-3	48 (4)
88	2.2b-2	21 (2)

Sources

Kuhn, Dieter. *The Age of Confucian Rule: The Song Transformation of China.* Cambridge: Harvard University Press, 2009.

Liu, James. *Reform in Sung China: Wang An-shih (1021–1086) and His New Policies.* Cambridge: Harvard University Press, 1959.

Meskill, John. *Wang An-shih: Practical Reformer?* Boston: D.C. Heath, 1963.

Pease, Jonathan. *From the Wellsweep to the Shallow Skiff: Life and Poetry of Wang Anshih.* Unpublished Ph.D. dissertation, 1986.

Twitchell, Denis, and Paul Smith. *The Cambridge History of China,* Vol. 5, *Part One: The Five Dynasties and Sung China.* Cambridge: Cambridge University Press, 2009.

Williamson, H. R. *Wang An-shih.* 2 vol. London: Arthur Probsthain, 1935.